The Battle's Sound

DRAKE'S DRUM *and* THE DRAKE FLAGS

Cynthia Gaskell Brown

DEVON BOOKS
Published in association with The National Trust
and the City of Plymouth Museum and Art Gallery

First published in Great Britain in 1996 by Devon Books

British Library Cataloguing in Publication Data
CIP Catalogue Record for this book is available from the British Library

ISBN 0 86114 899 1

DEVON BOOKS
Official Publisher to Devon County Council

Halsgrove House
Lower Moor Way
Tiverton
Devon EX16 6SS
Tel: 01884 243242
Fax: 01884 243325

Printed and bound in Great Britain by Ebenezer Baylis & Son Ltd

CONTENTS

1. 'The Embarkation of Henry VIII at Dover.' Painted c.1545 five years after Francis Drake was born. Similar flags and drums were still used in 1588 at the time of the Armada (see illustration 26). *The Royal Collection, Hampton Court, copyright Her Majesty the Queen.*

INTRODUCTION

This is an investigation of the engima of Drake's drum and the Drake flags. For more than two hundred years these remarkable treasures have been kept at Buckland Abbey, Devon, the home of the sixteenth-century adventurer and English hero, Sir Francis Drake. The drum was made famous and transformed into a symbol of English national pride in a poem by Sir Henry Newbolt in 1896. Since then the phrase 'Drake's Drum' has echoed in the imagination of English-speaking people around the world.

The Drum

The Drake drum is a large side drum of the sort generally used by foot soldiers in Europe during the sixteenth and seventeenth centuries. Rembrandt's famous painting 'The Night Watch' shows just such a drum and how it was carried.(6) Each company of soldiers at this time had its own drummer, flag bearer and fife player who together provided marching rhythms, signals for manoeuvres, a rallying point in battle and above all a focus for the pride and loyalty of the troops.

Side drums that can be dated before 1690 are of the greatest rarity in England. Only three are now known. One in the Royal Armouries in the Tower of London has been scientifically dated 1630–1645. Another was made in 1685 for the Oxford Volunteer Corps and is in All Souls College, Oxford. The Drake drum may be older than either of these.

The Flags

The eight ancient silk flags at Buckland Abbey are much less well known than the drum. Two of these Drake flags are Royal Standards blazoned in gold with the royal arms of Queen Elizabeth I of England. They are the only surviving English Standards of this age.

The other six flags are also unique. Made of crimson and white silk taffeta with gold emblems, they are a set of military Colours belonging to a Drake regiment. These certainly date back to the seventeenth century and might even be as old as the royal flags. Apart from the Drake flags it is thought that only five seventeenth century military Colours survive in England and none at all from the sixteenth century.

Ownership

Both the flags and the drum were offered in recent years to the government by the Drake family in lieu of death duties, and were privately appraised and valued.[1] The flags passed to the

National Trust in 1954 and the drum to Plymouth City Council in 1966.

The Enigma

Despite the rarity, importance and indeed fame of these Drake treasures no study of either the drum or the flags has ever been published. How old are they? Was the drum bought for the final expedition of the first Sir Francis Drake in 1595 or is it a relic of the seventeenth century? Do the flags belong with the drum? No reference to the drum or the flags appears in the family papers or in print until the eighteenth century. This account explores the evidence for their age and how they were made and used, and how the drum has acquired an almost religious significance in the last hundred years.

2. The Drake Drum at Buckland Abbey. *The National Trust.*

THE DRUM

How Was It Made?

The Drum Construction

The Drake drum is just over twenty-four inches (620 x 620mm) in height and the same in diameter. (**3a, b**) The shell or body of the drum is made of a very thin sheet of European walnut one-eighth of an inch (3mm) thick and eighty-eight inches (2235mm) long. The wood was cut across the full width of the tree and the lighter golden brown of the walnut sapwood can be seen at the top and bottom edges of the shell. (**4**) The ends of the sheet overlap by some ten inches (255mm) and are fixed together by dome headed brass nails with square shanks. These are arranged in an elaborate symmetrical pattern which includes a rosette around the single central air hole, and a somewhat blunted fleur-de-lys above and below. (**5a**)

The drum heads are ancient and probably made from calf skin. They are lapped round wooden flesh hoops held in place by modern counter hoops made of ash. The tension ropes and hide buffs which would originally have linked the top and bottom counter hoops and allowed the drum heads to be pulled tight are missing. Nor is there any evidence for fixings for the carrying strap from which the drum would have been slung at the side of the drummer's body.

The Batter Head

The upper, batter, head is now very uneven because of its continual exposure while on display in the Great Hall of Buckland Abbey. There are a few worm holes near the outer edge, but it now shows no sign of the characteristic marks in the centre of the skin which result from use.

The Snare Head

The lower, snare head is much better preserved. (**5c**) A small tear has been stitched together; this damage may have been caused by an attack on the drum by a lady with an umbrella in the 1930s! Most importantly the marks of the sheep gut snares which were originally stretched across the lower skin to enhance the tone and resonance of the drum are clearly visible. These snare marks interestingly consist of three not quite parallel lines, in effect a narrow elongated zig-zag. These are about three-eighths (9mm) of an inch apart.

Two of the marks extend almost the full width of the head, while the third stops well short of the edge. It has been suggested that early side drums always had two or four snares, increasing to four or six in the eighteenth century.[2] On the Drake drum it looks as though a single length of rather thick gut was run back and forth across the head three times and knotted off at each end.

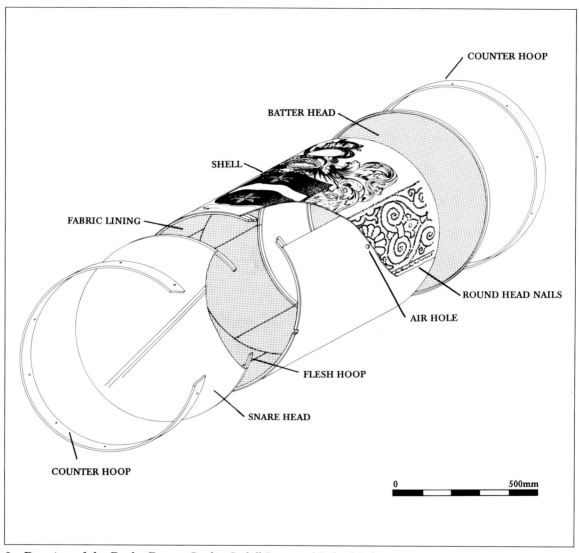

3a. Drawing of the Drake Drum. *Cynthia Gaskell Brown and Richard Fisher.*

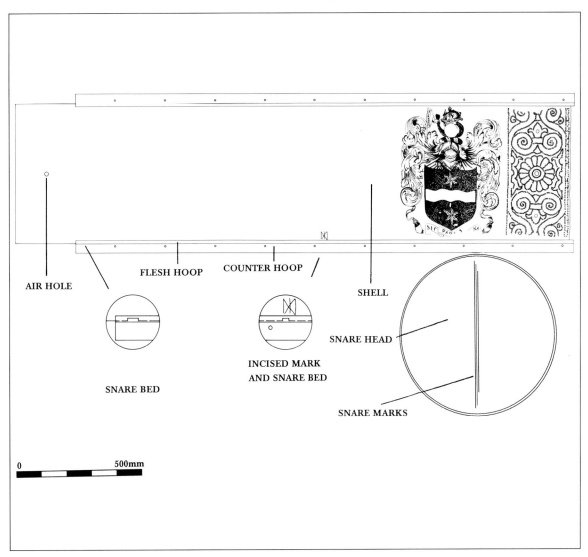

AIR HOLE

FLESH HOOP

COUNTER HOOP

SHELL

SNARE HEAD

SNARE BED

INCISED MARK AND SNARE BED

SNARE MARKS

0   500mm

3b. Drawing of the Drake Drum. *Cynthia Gaskell Brown and Richard Fisher.*

3

There is evidence for snare beds, the shallow depressions cut in the edge of the wooden shell which allowed the snares to fit tightly against the drum head. Although the head of the drum cannot now be removed these depressions can just be felt through the skin. One snare bed lies in line with the edge of the nailed join and is about three-quarters of an inch (19mm) wide; the other diametrically opposite is about half an inch (9mm) wide. The snare marks on the drum head are no longer aligned with the snare beds, doubtless because the head was removed and replaced during the repairs done this century.

Damage and Repair

The counter hoops which hold the drum heads in place are modern replacements and are made of ash. These are thought to be reasonably accurate copies of the originals and have ten angled holes for the tension rope. The circumstances of the repair and cleaning of the drum were explained in a letter written to the then Curator of Plymouth Museum, Alex Cumming, in 1951.[3]

4. **The Drake Drum.** *Plymouth City Museum.*

> *Plymouth*
> *14th August 1951*
>
> *Dear Sir*
> *As Buckland Abbey has now been officially opened and is arousing considerable interest, especially in the West Country, it may be of interest to you to know that my late husband, J.C. Passmore did a lot of work at Buckland Abbey. In 1909 he was employed by the late Lady Elliot Drake to clean and restore the carved screen in the Hall. Whilst my husband was working on the screen, Lady Elliot Drake decided to have Drake's Drum removed from the position it occupied in the Hall and have it placed on brackets over the Hall door.*
> *She asked an employee to put the Drum on a table and in doing so the hoops at the top and bottom of the Drum fell off as they were riddled with woodworm, Lady Drake was very upset and asked my husband what could be done. He told her he could make two new hoops, and also suggested immersing the Drum in paraffin oil to kill any woodworm or grub which might be in it. After the Drum had been immersed in paraffin for sometime, my*

5a. The join, air vent and nail pattern.

5b. The back of the drum with incised mark.

5c. The snare head with triple snare marks.

5d. Detail of incised mark, later damage and wormholes.

husband noticed colours slightly showing on the Drum, he then proceeded to clean the Drum, and in doing so Drake's coat of arms, and other designs re-appeared which had been obscured by the dirt and grime of many years. When the Drum was perfectly clean my husband then made and fixed the hoops which are now on the Drum, needless to say, Lady Drake was delighted with the result, as she had no idea that there was any design or Coat of Arms on the Drum.

I hope this information will be of interest to you.

Yours faithfully
M. Passmore (Mrs)

The damage caused by the breaking of the original counter hoops and by woodworm was confined to the sapwood at the upper and lower edges of the drum. An additional strengthening ring has been added to the inside lower edge of the shell and the whole interior lined with two strips of beige fabric which is carefully gored so that the fabric lies flat in the curved shell. This work was done c.1952 when the drum was passed to the workshop of Harris's of Plymouth for conservation.[4] Examination with an endoscope in 1993 confirmed that the lining lies over all the nails and strengthening rings inside.[5] The shell of an eighteenth century long drum, preserved in Exeter Museum, is also lined although the canvas in that drum runs underneath the internal strengthening rings and is presumably part of the original construction. The only other noticeable change to Drake's drum is the slightly rippled profile of the shell caused by gradual warping over the centuries.

Decoration

The drum has a distinctive version of the Drake coat of arms painted on the polished golden brown shell. (**4**) Apart from the elaborate rosette pattern of the nails there is one other feature on the outside of the drum. This is on the plain side opposite the join and is a mark near the lower edge which has never previously been considered, nor copied on to replicas of the drum. (**5b**) Roughly incised, it consists of three vertical lines overlain by a cross. It may represent the Roman number XIII. (**5d**) A search for marks on other drums has brought to light a double 'V' stamped onto the leather carrying case for a tabor c.1545, which was recovered from the wreck of Henry VIII's ship the *Mary Rose* ; while the 18th century Exeter drum mentioned above has a roughly incised 'N' on the wooden shell. All three marks were added to the drums after manufacture. It seems likely that they are inventory marks which would allow drums to be issued to the right company.

THE DRUM

How Was It Used?

By the sixteenth century large side drums were widely used by armies in Europe.[6] This practice seems to have been copied from the mercenary regiments of Switzerland where drum and fife players had formed Guilds as early as 1332. Ralph Smith, an Englishman writing in the 1550s, explained the duties of a military drummer. These included teaching the company 'the sound of march, alarm, approach, assault, battle, retreat and skirmish'. But as well as this drummers were regarded as negotiators 'for often times they be sent to parley with their enemies, to summon their forts or towns, to redeem and conduct prisoners and divers other messages, which of necessity required language'.[7]

When acting as negotiator the drummer was vulnerable and in these circumstances it was thought dishonourable to strike or wound him. This special status is vividly shown by an episode during the attack by the English fleet on the Spanish town of La Coruña in 1589:

The same day the (Spanish) Generall ... caused the Towne to be summoned: in which summons they of the Towne shot at our drum; immediately after that there was one hanged over the wall and a parle desired: wherein they gave us to understand that the man was he that shot at the drum before.[8]

The close association of drummer and ensign bearer and their crucial positions at the head of companies while marching and in the centre of formations during battle is plainly seen in contemporary illustrations, such as the diagrams of drill practice for Henry VIII's army. (7) The characteristic stance of the military drummer is well known from Rembrandt's painting. (6) Drums in use and being carried about can be seen in the 1545 picture of Henry VIII's army on the ill-fated day of the sinking of the *Mary Rose*. (8, 9)

The records of Sir Francis Drake's own adventures show clearly that drums and drumming were an essential part of discipline and strategy both aboard ship and during raids ashore. Drake's first successful raid on Spanish treasure being brought from Peru to the Caribbean was near the town of Nombre de Dios in 1573. The description of this raid shows how drumming was used to intimidate an enemy:

himself (Drake) with the rest would passe up the broad street into the market place with the sound of Drum and Trumpets... The inhabitants stood amazed at so strange a sight marvellinge, by reason of our Drums and Trumpets sounding in so sundry places, that we had beene farre greater number than we were.[9]

6. 'The Night Watch', Rembrandt, 1642. A Dutch drum with tension ropes, buffs, geometric nail pattern and snares. *Rijksmuseum, Amsterdam.*

During the privateering war which Drake led against the Spanish cities in the West Indies in 1585–86 drums are again clearly identified as a key part of military strategy. The fleet consisted

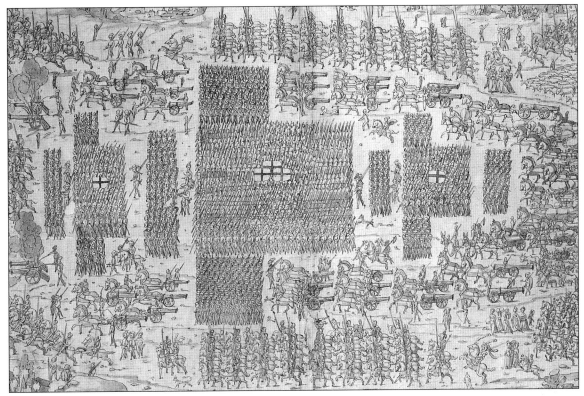

7. Side drums and ensigns, c.1540 in diagrams of manoeuvres for Henry VIII's army. *British Library Cott. Aug. III, 168–170.*

of twenty two ships with over two thousand men aboard, including twelve companies of soldiers. In 1586 the English fleet reached the West Indies and lay off the Spanish city of San Domingo. Carleill disembarked eight hundred soldiers:

whereupon the 800 men cutting between them (the Spanish) and the town fell upon their backs and striking

up their drums, displaying ensigns and such things: which so amazed them that there were scattered, killed and spoiled in a moment near 6000.[10]

Drums were also as important on board ship in the sixteenth century for calls to action, to accompany floggings and for burial at sea. But they were often used more cheerfully along with trumpets and fifes

8. Side drum with royal arms on the shell being carried on the drummer's back; 'The Encampment of the English Forces at Portsmouth', c.1545. *Society of Antiquaries, London.*

9. Side drummer with ensigns: 'The Encampment of the English Forces at Portsmouth', c.1545. *Society of Antiquaries, London.*

to honour visiting commanders and to help provide music at formal meals. The splendid painting showing the Embarkation of Henry VIII at Dover in 1520 (painted c. 1545) has side drums in the two small boats carrying dignatories out to the great ship *Henri Grâce À Dieu*. (**10a, b**). Here they are clearly providing the stroke for the oarsmen on this great royal occasion.

Buying Drums

In August 1595 Sir Francis Drake and Sir John Hawkins sailed from Plymouth on their final expedition to raid Spanish treasure ships in the Caribbean. In the long and detailed list of equipment bought for this voyage is the item; 'Sundry instrumentes of music for 8 musicians and nine trumpeters £14.11.0'.[11] After Drake's death the following January 'a cheste of instrumentes of musicke' was removed from his ship the *Defiance* which contained 'a lute, hobboyes, sagbutes, Cornettes & orpharions, bandora & such like'.[12] Aboard the commander's ships the officers and gentlemen adventurers had relaxed in some style.

Further down the list and itemised quite separately between fishing lines, sounding leads and tar is the purchase of thirteen drums:[13]

DRUMS	£. s. d.
2 at 30 shillings the piece and	
11 bought by agreement at £14.	17. 0. 0

These thirteen drums, two of which were clearly larger or more elaborate than the rest, were bought for an expedition of twenty-seven ships,

10a, b. Drum marking time for oarsmen; "The Embarkation of Henry VIII at Dover", c.1545. *The Royal Collection, Hampton Court, copyright Her Majesty the Queen.*

which effectively sailed as two separate squadrons. They had with them under the command of Sir Thomas Baskerville rather fewer than a thousand soldiers who formed twelve companies.[14]

Were the two more expensive drums perhaps for use on Drake and Hawkins' own ships, the *Defiance* and the *Garland*? Is the strange mark on the Drake drum at Buckland Abbey perhaps the number XIII? Could the drum indeed be one of the thirteen bought for that last sad voyage during which both Sir Francis Drake and Sir John Hawkins died of dysentry?

THE DRUM
How Old Is It?

One of the most fascinating challenges presented by any rare antique object is proving its authenticity and dating it precisely. Very occasionally there is an actual date or maker's mark on it. There are for instance five ancient Swiss side drums in the extensive collections in the Historisches Museum, Basel, which have sixteenth and seventeenth century dates painted on their shells.[15] (**11**) But there is no date painted on the Drake drum.

Another more common means is to use evidence from family papers, contemporary account books, wills and inventories. The side drum preserved in All Souls College, Oxford can be dated this way. It was bought by a Fellow of the college, Leopold Finch, for the Oxford Volunteer Corps which he raised to fight against the Duke of Monmouth's rebellion in 1685. On disbandment the drum was placed in the Bursar's office where it has remained ever since.[16] (**15**)

Unfortunately the Drake drum cannot be dated by this means either. There are no known references to the drum in family wills or papers in the sixteenth and seventeenth centuries.

It is not mentioned in a list of family valuables hastily dispersed amongst friends in 1682 by Sir Francis Drake (3rd Baronet 1647–1718) when he was out of favour with the future King James II.[17]

11. Swiss side drum bearing the date 1575 (h640 x d510mm). *Historisches Museum, Basel.*

Nor is it in the small Drake notebook of 1778 which lists the flags and other Drake family treasures, as well as household linen and silver.[18]

Historic Records

The first specific reference to a drum being at Buckland Abbey does not appear until 1799 when the traveller George Lipscomb published *A Journey into Cornwall...* Writing of Buckland Abbey he says 'The sword of this great man (Francis Drake) together with an old drum which circuited the world with him are still preserved in the house'.

After this first guide-book entry nineteenth-century writers frequently mention the Drake relics: 'the sword, and an old drum' in 1803; 'his sword, drum and black letter Bible' in 1829; 'his ship drum' in 1832. These traveller's accounts however do no more than prove that the drum has been kept at Buckland Abbey since the end of the eighteenth century and belonged to the Drake family. So other ways of dating the drum have to be explored.

Technical Possibilities

Tree ring dating was successfully used on the drum in the Armouries of the Tower of London in 1974. This is a large side drum which had been converted in the nineteenth century into a long drum and painted with the monogram of King William IV.[19] (**12, 13**) Precise counts of the number and width of growth rings on the edge of the drum shell provided a date of 1630–45.

Excellent sequences have now been established for dating oak in Europe and some seventy-five stringed instruments made of German spruce

12. The side drum, Royal Armouries, London. Dated by dendrochronology to 1630–45, later converted to a long drum with the monogram of William IV (1830–37) painted horizontally.

have been precisely dated by this technique.

The Drake drum is made of walnut.[20] Unfortunately growth rings in walnut, as in poplar

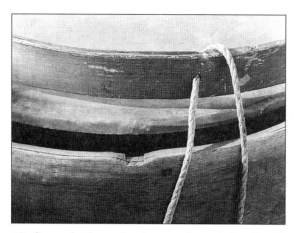

13. Snare bed on the lower edge of the Royal Armouries drum.

and lime trees, are very difficult to distinguish and reference sequences cannot be built up. So dendrochronology cannot be used to date the drum.

The other potentially useful technique, that of radio-carbon dating, is much less precise than dendrochronology. Radio-carbon dates always carry a margin of error that is relatively wide, and in the historic period this often means that the date cannot be resolved. The difficulty of taking an uncontaminated sample of wood of the right size without damaging the drum is also a problem, which means this technique is not suitable.

However, comparison with surviving drums, with drawings, paintings and early written descriptions, as well as the analysis of the decoration of the Drake drum can all be used to try to solve the mystery of its date.

The Dromster & Fyfe..

14. An English drummer and fife player c.1590. *Pepys Library, Cambridge.*

Size

The oldest account of the art of drumming is by the French writer Thoinot Arbeau who in 1588 describes a side drum as 'two and a half feet' in each dimension. This large 'square' proportion is shown in the woodcut of an English drummer of 1590 (**14**). The largest side drums in the well-dated Swiss collection in Basel also belong to the sixteenth century (although these are not quite so square as the north European drums) and are between twenty-one and twenty-five inches (550–640mm) in height.

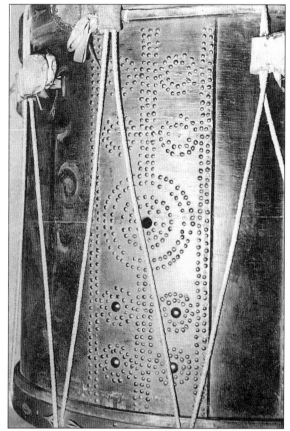

15. The side drum of the Oxford Volunteer Corps, c.1685 (h536 x d520mm). *Maurice Byrne.*

In the seventeeth century side drums get noticeably smaller. The Royal Armouries drum of 1630-45 is some twenty-two inches in height (572 x 554mm) and the All Souls College drum of 1685 is twenty-one inches (536 x 520mm). The Swiss seventeenth-century drums are almost all even smaller. By the eighteenth century British drums such as John Middleton's regimental drum in Edinburgh Castle are only about sixteen inches (380mm) in height.

On the basis of size the Drake drum certainly fits into the sixteenth-century range, and with the exception of a Swiss drum of 1575, is much the largest instrument surviving.

The Pattern of Nails
The very distinctive and elaborate pattern of nails which decorate the join of the shell of the Drake drum are not matched on any actual drum or painting. An almost standard simple arrangement of circles and lines was used in the seventeenth century, for instance on the drum shown in 'The Night Watch' and the drum in the portrait of Charles I, 1650 (**6, 16**) The fleur-de-lys and scrolls of the Drake drum on the other hand do have the feel of some of the patterns used in Tudor fabrics, for example in the clothes worn in the portrait of Elizabeth I by W. Stertes in the Royal Collection.

The Coat of Arms
The drum is decorated in the traditional manner with the coat of arms of the Drake family which is painted quite thinly on to the wood and shows no sign of alteration or touching in. (**4**) Francis

16. An English side drum with a simple nail pattern round the air vent. 'Portrait of Charles I and Sir Edward Waller', c.1650. *National Portrait Gallery, London.*

Drake was knighted aboard his ship the *Golden Hind* by Queen Elizabeth I in April 1581. A painting on vellum of Drake's armorial bearings was issued two months later by Robert Cook, Clarenceaux King of Arms. **(17)**

On the drum the coat of arms is painted with the helmet on the crest facing forward, with the visor open. Although sixteenth century versions of the Drake coat of arms vary, all of them show the crest with the helmet facing to the left, with the visor closed. **(18, 19)** On the other hand the Drake arms in plasterwork over the Tower Room fireplace in Buckland Abbey, dated 1655, has the helmet facing forward just as it is on the drum. **(20)**

17. The Drake Grant of Arms, 1581. *Private collection.*

18. Variants of the Drake Coat of Arms: Paper impression of Sir Francis Drake's personal seal on the codicil to his will, 27 January 1595/96, his arms quartered with wyverns. *Plymouth City Museum.*

The style of the arms on the drum was examined by Somerset Herald, at the College of Arms in 1993.[21] In his opinion the painting of the coat of arms dates between 1611 and 1679. During this period a book by John Guillim 'The Display of Heraldrie' advised that knights helmets should be drawn facing forward, and it became quite common to do so. Sir Francis Drake used a personal seal in which the arms granted to him in 1581 were quartered with wyverns (or dragons).[22] An impression of this on paper can be seen on the codicil to his will which was signed and sealed by him at sea the day before his death, in January 1595/96. Another version of this appears in the

19. Coat of arms on portrait of Sir Francis Drake, c.1581; the helmet facing left. *National Maritime Museum.*

20. Buckland Abbey plasterwork, 1655: the coat of arms above the fireplace, with the helmet facing forward, as on the drum. *The National Trust.*

engraved portrait of Drake by Hondius, c.1590. Both these are on show at Buckland Abbey. It seems likely that if the drum had indeed been personally associated with Drake, this particular version of his arms would have been used.

However there may be another explanation. The Royal Armouries drum was left plain until the nineteenth century when the arms of William

IV were added to the shell. Could the Drake drum too have been a plain sixteenth-century instrument or one with a much worn coat of arms, which was refurbished in the seventeenth century?

Conclusion

The dating of the Drake drum is ambiguous. The seventeenth-century style of the coat of arms is at odds with all the evidence for a sixteenth century date, which includes the large size, the square proportions, the uniquely elaborate nail patterns and the possible connection of the roughly cut number thirteen incised on the drum shell with

21. Sir Francis Drake, c.1581. *National Portrait Gallery.*

the thirteen drums bought for Sir Francis Drake's last voyage to the Carribean in 1595.

The drum is nevertheless unique and probably the oldest side drum surviving in Britain.

THE DRAKE FLAGS

The eight ancient flags which formerly belonged to the Drake family were given to the National Trust in 1954.[23] The earliest family record of these flags is in a list written on four pages at the back of a small eighteenth-century notebook belonging to Sir Francis Henry Drake, the 5th Baronet.[24] This is a simple inventory of family valuables and linen which were at that time kept in eight boxes and trunks at Buckland Abbey and it is dated May 1778 and July 1779.

The first page begins with the contents of a box containing: 'The first Sir Francis Drakes Plate given him by Queen Elizabeth'. The second box held the family's Elizabethan jewels and miniature portraits. Two other boxes held silver cutlery, cruets and candlesticks, and four further chests and trunks held linen. The list ends:

In a Lesser Trunk
Four fine Damask Tablecloths. F.D.1.2.3.4.
1750
Four Do. Diaper. F.D.5.6.7.8.
Six very fine Diaper Breakfast Cloths.
Two Chintz Window Curtains.
Old Sir Francis Drake's Sash and Cap.
His silk Colours, in Number eight, as follow –

The rest of the page is unfortunately blank and the details of the flags were never added. What is of interest is the description as 'Colours' showing that in the eighteenth century these flags were quite clearly considered to be military flags, belonging to the first Sir Francis.

Because the flags were stored with the family linen they have been preserved in remarkably fine condition. In 1950 the Royal School of Needlework restored and mounted four of the flags on canvas. These four flags (the two Royal Standards and the Colours bearing a sphere and a pile wavy) have since 1952 been on show at Buckland Abbey.

The Royal Standards

The two most splendid flags are Royal Standards bearing the arms of Queen Elizabeth I. The larger flag is seven feet square (2070 x 2070mm) with the lions and fleur-de-lys blazoned in gold leaf on red and turquoise-blue Spanish silk damasks. (22) The emblems are outlined and have details in black, and the lions have blue claws and nostrils and red tongues. At least two highly skilled painters were involved as some of the lions look much more amiable than others. Each quarter of the flag is made of two pieces of damask joined horizontally with self-enclosed seams. The patterns on the two damasks are very similar but not identical and are carefully matched at the joins. The green and white silk fringe was restored in 1950 when the silk sleeve to

22. The Drake Flags: The Royal Standard with the arms of Elizabeth I on Spanish silk damasks. *The National Trust.*

22

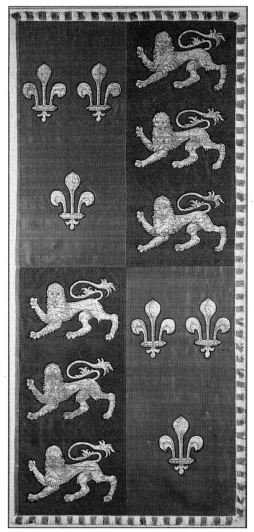

23. The Royal Standard with the arms of Elizabeth I on plain silk. *The National Trust.*

24. The lion from the smaller Royal Standard. *The National Trust.*

take the flagstaff was created in place of a row of eyelets which are visible in old photographs.

The other Standard is an unusual shape, a narrow upright rectangle, seven feet high but only two feet ten inches wide (2070 x 864mm). Made of plain red and blue silks, this has the emblems painted in the same way as on the larger standard although the lions are more thickset to fit the narrow width. (**23**). This flag differs from all the others in having a strip of canvas containing eleven eyelets along the hoist which would allow it to be laced to the flagstaff. Lacing flags in this way was in later centuries a distinctly naval habit. These elaborate and beautifully made flags may well have been painted in the workshops of the Queen's serjeant-painter.[25]

They are perhaps mementoes of the glittering occasion in April 1581 when Queen Elizabeth I knighted Francis Drake aboard his ship the *Golden*

25. Royal Standards in use. *The Royal Collection, Hampton Court, copyright Her Majesty The Queen.*

Hind at Deptford. However Drake certainly used the Royal Standards on other occasions, particularly on his expeditions which had formal royal support. His privateering war in the West Indies in 1585–86 was carefully recorded in drawings published two years later. These clearly show Drake's ship flying the Royal Standard at the stern, with the St George's flag of England at the mast head; and the use of horizontal and diagonal striped flags not only at the stern of the other ships in the fleet, but also by companies of soldiers ashore.

Even more specific are the accounts for the final voyage of Drake and Hawkins in 1595 which list the purchase of:[26]

FLAGS	£ . s. d
4 at 60/–, gilt her majesty's arms upon silk; 30 of St George at 16/8d each	37 0 0
STREAMERS	
3 at £8, with her majesty's badges in silver and gold and 80 at 25/–	124 0 0
ENSIGNS	
26 of 11 and 12 breadths at 46/– each	60 0 0

The specification of 11 and 12 breadths for the ensigns strongly suggests striped flags. If the breadth was of eleven inches (as recorded by Samuel Pepys in the seventeenth century) and allowing for seams this would make the flags at least nine feet square. Given this large size it may be that these ensigns were for shipboard use rather than as soldiers colours, although no other flags are listed.

The picture of the Ark Royal, 1588, shows how these various flags and streamers were worn. (**26**) The Royal Standard is on the main mast; a square flag with the Tudor rose and two St George's flags are on the other masts; and four streamers fly from cross-trees and bow-sprit. Lord Howard of Effingham's own coat of arms on a square flag are shown at deck level with a drummer standing next to the fore-mast.

While very large flags were made for use at sea, a range of sizes would have been needed for smaller ships, and the pinnaces which ferried crews to and from shore.[25] The smaller Drake Standard may perhaps have been used this way; and the square flag could well have been his own 'amphibious' flag.

There is no doubt that these two Standards date from the reign of Elizabeth I, for on the accession of James I in 1603 the coat of arms of England was altered to include symbols for Scotland and Ireland.

The Drake Colours

The other six Drake flags are of quite a different character to the Royal Standards, but are just as rare and much more puzzling. (**27**) Made of crimson silk taffeta, five of them have a white taffeta cross running from edge to edge of the flags, in effect a reversed St George's Cross. Five of the flags also bear distinctive gold symbols; an eight-pointed star (étoille), a streamer (pile wavy) a sphere (bezant), a belled falcon, and a fleur-de-lys. These are of gold leaf, with the details painted in sepia, and shadow lines in black.

26. The 'Ark Royal', 1588. Admiral Lord Howard's flagship wearing at the mastheads flags with the Royal badge, the Royal coat of arms, and the St George's cross, and streamers in several places. His own flag is displayed on deck with a side drummer to the right. *British Museum.*

Each flag is just under seven feet square (2070 x 2070mm) with a linen lined sleeve to take a wooden staff which tapered towards the top of the flag. The flags were tied to the staff by the twelve-inch-long pair of red and white tassled cords which are sewn at the top of each flag, and secured by tapes at the bottom. A narrow taffeta tape survives on one colour.

The flags are made of four pieces of crimson silk joined to the white silk cross with self enclosed seams. The one flag without a white cross has a horizontal seam in the centre. All the flags are

26

The Drake Colours
The National Trust.

27a. Colonel's flag.

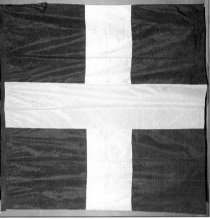

b. Lt. Colonel's flag.

c. Sergeant-Major's flag.

d, e, f, Captain's flags.

slightly gathered at the top where the sheet is stitched to the sleeve and all show signs of use, with small darns, patches and tears, and wear on the gold devices.

Sixteenth Century Evidence

The design of these six flags is puzzling. In the late sixteenth century ships often used ensigns with multi-coloured horizontal stripes, along with the national flag, the St George's Cross; while on land the need to distinguish one company of soldiers from another was met by having flags with complex patterns of stripes and crosses.

Sometime between the 1580s and 1625 a formal system of showing military rank on flags became accepted. The system is first mentioned in Markham's book *The Soldiers Accidence* in 1625, where the use of devices taken from the crests and arms of the officers is advised. Extensive records and sketches from the period of the English Civil Wars, and five surviving Civil War flags, show that by the 1640s most regiments and Trained Bands used an organised set of symbols.[27] **(28)**

During the Civil War, however, the St George's cross was confined to the top left quarter (canton) of the flag, not spread over the whole sheet as in the sixteenth century, as it was to be again after the Restoration in 1661.

The Drake flags fit neatly enough into the ranking system described in 1625. The Colonel's flag is plain with a family device in the centre; the star of Sir Francis Drake's arms. The Lieutenant-Colonel had a plain cross; the Major a cross with a 'pile wavy' in the top left corner. Each of the three captain's flags has a cross with a symbol in the corner: a belled falcon, a fleur-de-lys, and a sphere (bezant). The flags clearly are a set of Colours for a regiment of six companies. What is odd about them is that the cross is not in fact a St George's cross – red on white – but has the colours reversed.

Could the practice of showing rank and family allegiance on militia colours go back as far as Drake's time? After 1573 Queen Elizabeth's commissioners began to enforce the selection of men from the County Militia for regular training. This was a response to the increasing tension between England and Spain which culminated in the summer of 1588 with the arrival of the Spanish Armada.[28]

What had been a rather casual amateur militia became increasingly organised and muster lists naming officers and soldiers were returned. Drake's strong political, business and property interests in Plymouth in the years after his voyage around the world and his knighthood in 1581 (he was Mayor of Plymouth that year) make it possible that he or his brother Thomas were involved in the Plymouth militia in the 1580s.

The west part of Plymouth fell within the Stannary of Tavistock at that time and the Tinners had jealously guarded the tradition of raising their own militia. They might perhaps have had distinctive flags but there are no surviving sixteenth century records for the Devon or Stannary militia save for one year, 1569, long before Drake could have been involved. It would seem that no documentary or visual records survive to help resolve the question of the design of militia flags in the sixteenth century.

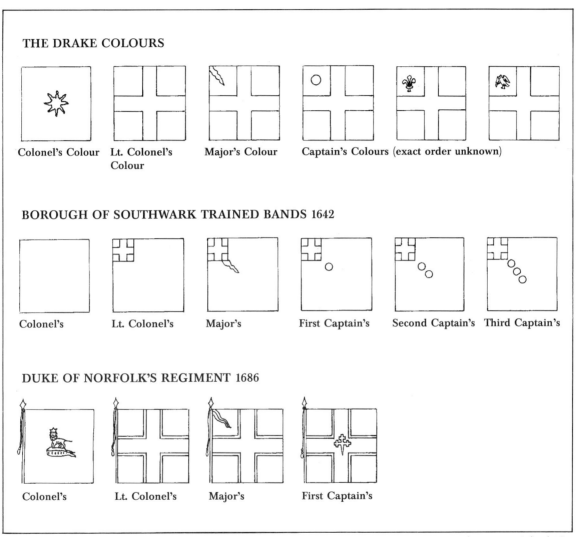

THE DRAKE COLOURS

Colonel's Colour | Lt. Colonel's Colour | Major's Colour | Captain's Colours (exact order unknown)

BOROUGH OF SOUTHWARK TRAINED BANDS 1642

Colonel's | Lt. Colonel's | Major's | First Captain's | Second Captain's | Third Captain's

DUKE OF NORFOLK'S REGIMENT 1686

Colonel's | Lt. Colonel's | Major's | First Captain's

28. The Drake Colours compared with Civil War and late seventeenth century flags (not to scale). (*After Peachey and Prince; Milne*).

29

Seventeenth Century Evidence

Are there later members of the Drake family who might have carried these Colours? There are only seven surviving lists of militia officers for Devon or the Stannaries up to 1638. The second Sir Francis Drake (1st Baronet 1588-1637) does not appear in any of these.[30] A regiment led by Col. Sir John Drake, of Ashe in East Devon, does appear in 1633, but the Drakes of Ashe were a quite separate family with their own coat of arms showing wyverns (dragons) and axes which cannot be connected to the Buckland flags.[31]

With the coming of the English Civil War, Sir Francis Drake (2nd Baronet 1617-1662), raised the Plymouth Regiment of Horse for the Parliamentary cause. Horse regiments used pennants with designs quite different from the Drake Colours so that no connection can be made there. Only at the end of the seventeenth century does a Drake appear as Colonel in the militia lists.[32] This was Sir Francis Henry Drake (3rd Baronet 1647-1718).

In 1697 the list notes:

Sir Francis Drake, Bart. Col: *Josias Calmady, Esq,* Lt-Col; *Courtenay Croker, Esq,* Major; *William Dyer; John Fountain, William Ibert, Esqs,* Captains. *6 Companies, 860 men.*

By this date army regiments have the St George's cross filling the whole flag, often as a red cross with white edging set against another background colour.

While the ranking system continued in use in the late seventeenth century, the Captain's devices were placed in the centre of the cross, or their rank shown by numerals in the top left canton.[33] **(28)**

However, no link can be found to match the symbols shown on the Drake Colours and the crests or family arms of the men on the 1697 militia list.

Conclusion

The Drake Colours are idiosyncratic but almost certainly pre-date the Civil War. They are seven feet square, the same size as the larger of the sixteenth-century Royal Standards in contrast to seventeenth-century flags which tend to be rectangular and smaller.[34]

The use of individual symbols on the captain's flags fits with Markham's early seventeenth-century advice. The Colours could well be older than this and contemporary with the first Sir Francis Drake. They are outstanding in quality, remarkably preserved and are the only surviving set of early military flags in England.

LEGEND AND MYTH

Sir Francis Drake was famous in his own lifetime as the first Englishman to circumnavigate the world between 1577–1580 and as the scourge of Spanish treasure ships in the Caribbean Seas.[35]

In the west of England his heroic standing in the eyes of local people was particularly reinforced in 1588 when, as the English fleet engaged the Spanish Armada off the coast of Devon, Drake captured the Spanish flagship *Nuestra Senora del Rosario* and sent it as a prize into Dartmouth. It was the only prize taken and its captors brought the first news local people had of the progress of the battle.

In the account of Sir Francis Drake's final voyage to the Caribbean written by his young kinsman Thomas Maynard in 1595 there is a character sketch of Drake at the end of his life that bears the stamp of reality, and reflects his weaknesses as well as his strengths:

A man of great spirit and fitt to undertake matters... better able to conduct forces and discreetly to governe in conducting them to places where service was to be done than to command in the executions thereof. But assuredly his very name was a greate terror to the enemie in all those partes [the West Indies] havinge hearetofore done many things in those countries to his honorable fame and profitt. But entringe into them as the childe of fortune it may be that his selfe-willed and peremtorie command was doubted. And that caused her majestie (as should seeme) to joyne Sir John Hawkins in equall commission.[36]

29. Portrait of Sir Francis Drake, c.1580. *National Maritime Museum.*

But Drake's personality and exploits very quickly became viewed as part of a 'golden age'. By 1626 his nephew, the second Sir Francis Drake, had published a booklet *Sir Francis Drake Revived: Calling upon this Dull or Effeminate Age to follow his Noble Steps for Gold and Silver.* Alongside this hero worship, legend and myths soon developed.

Drake the Magician

The 'great terror' inspired in Drake's enemies throughout his life caused the Spaniards to transform his name into *El Draco* – the Dragon – and Spanish prisoners taken during the Armada fight in 1588 reported him to be in league with the devil. In an age when Drake, in common with most people, took witchcraft and necromancy seriously, he had himself during his voyage of circumnavigation in 1578 accused his fellow officer Thomas Doughty of being a conjuror and Doughty's brother a witch.

So it is perhaps not surprising to find that by the early nineteenth century folk tales attribute magical powers to Sir Francis Drake. One story tells how after playing bowls on Plymouth Hoe while waiting for the Spanish Armada, Drake chopped up a block of wood and threw the fragments off Devil's Point into Plymouth Sound. There they instantly turned into fire ships which defeated the Armada.

Drake's astute political skill which led to the construction of the leat for Plymouth's water supply in 1590, is transformed in another tale into powers as a wizard in which guise he caused the water to flow magically behind his horse as he rode from Dartmoor to Plymouth. Other stories are less clearly connected with real events but are linked to his name. They fall into familiar categories of common folk tales – ghosts at Buckland Abbey; headless horses pulling a carriage near Tavistock; and a building at Buckland Abbey put up in three nights by the devil.[37]

'Drakes Drum'

Only one reference to the drum occurs in these earlier tales, published by Robert Hunt in 1871:

Even now – as old Betty Donithorne, formerly the housekeeper at Buckland Abbey told me – if the warrior hears the drum which hangs in the hall of the Abbey and which accompanied him around the world, he rises and has a revel.

This is very different in character to the accounts, which are still repeated, that tell of the sound of the drum being heard beating when England is in danger; or the other strand of anecdotes which connect the drum with bad luck.[38]

These stories emerge in the late nineteenth century at the height of Victorian self-confidence in the British Empire and pride in the British Navy. Historical fiction such as Kingsley's *Westward Ho!* and Henty's *Under Drake's Flag* were matched by dramatic narrative paintings.

The drama and splendour of the late Victorian paintings 'The Surrender' (1889) (**30**) and 'The Burial of Admiral Drake' (1906) (**31**) match the mood that created the statues of Drake put up in Tavistock and on Plymouth Hoe in 1884, and the enthusiasm that marked the celebration of the Tercentenary of the Armada in Plymouth in 1888.

30. 'The Surrender' by John Seymour Lucas, 1889. *Plymouth City Museum.*

Stories about the drum itself clearly start after the publication of Sir Henry Newbolt's poem in January 1896. Although by this time accurate historical research was available in print (Julian Corbett's biography of Drake appeared in 1890) the poem reflects, not scholarship, but a romantic and chauvinistic view of the Elizabethan age which is well described by Newbolt himself. In his memoirs he notes how:

While a young barrister and contributing occasional verses to London journals, early in 1896 the Kaiser Wilhelm had made a threatening move, and it was announced that as a proof of our readiness to meet a serious challenge a Special Service Squadron would be sent to sea at once. I had in my drawer some verses which I had written with the title 'Drake's Drum' more than a month before – early in December, 1895. I posted them to the Editor, Sidney Low, as possibly appropriate to the present moment, and on the evening of 15th January I had the singular pleasure of seeing in every street as I walked home from Lincoln's Inn the placards of the St. James Gazette bearing the two words only, in enormous capitals: as it were the beat of the Drum made visible. The sense of fatefulness was redoubled next day when we read that the Flying Squadron had gone to sea with the Revenge *for flagship and Captain Drake as commander of the Marines.*

The poem was set to music in 1904 by Sir Charles Villiers Stanford, Professor of Music at Cambridge, and with its catchy words and stirring rhythm became enormously popular.

DRAKE'S DRUM
Sir Henry Newbolt

Drake he's in his hammock an' a thousand miles away,
(Capten, art tha sleepin' there below?)
Slung atween the round shot in Nombre Dios Bay,
An' dreaming arl the time o' Plymouth Hoe.
Yarnder lumes the Island, yarnder lie the ships,
Wi' sailor lads a dancin' heel-an-toe,
An' the shore-lights flashin', an' the night-tide dashin',
He sees et arl so plainly as he saw et long ago.

Drake he was a Devon man, an' ruled the Devon seas,
(Capten, art tha sleepin' there below?)
Rovin' tho' his death fell, he went wi' heart at ease,
An' dreamin' arl the time o' Plymouth Hoe.
'Take my drum to England, hang et by the shore,
Strike et when your powder's runnin' low;
If the Dons sight Devon, I'll quite the port o'Heaven,

An' drum them up the Channel as we drummed them long ago.'

Drake he's in his hammock till the great Armadas come,
(Capten, art tha sleepin' there below?)
Slung atween the round shot, listenin' for the drum,
An' dreamin' arl the time o' Plymouth Hoe.
Call him on the deep sea, call him up the Sound,
Call him when ye sail to meet the foe;
Where the old trade's plyin' an' the old flag flyin'
They shall find him ware an' waking', as they found him long ago!

It is only after the song became well known that the Drake's Drum stories emerge. At the surrender of the German fleet at Scapa Flow, in 1918, naval officers aboard the *Royal Oak*, a Westcountry ship, believed they heard the beating of a drum which could not be traced, and which only ceased when the German flag was hauled down. A similar story was repeated in the Second World War in 1940 by soldiers in Hampshire, where two officers on the coast heard a drum beating a distinct pattern; the drummer was not found, despite thorough checks over a wide area.

Stories of bad luck and Drake's Drum revolve around HMS *Devonshire* which was carrying a silver replica of the Drake drum in 1929 and are recorded in letters and newspaper cuttings held by Plymouth Museum. One letter records how it was felt that 'only a cleric should touch it; and when a seaman named Cooper did so, he became ill. Later the ship hit the harbour wall, and on its

31. The Burial of Drake by Thomas Davidson, 1906. *Plymouth City Museum.*

second trip the ship caught fire. The crew refused to sail until the replica was removed'.

These stories which transform the drum into an icon with a life of its own are notably connected with the Royal Navy and the Westcountry, where the exploits of Drake and his characteristics of bravery, patriotism and resolution have remained part of the inheritance of the Royal Navy and the local community in Devon and Cornwall for over four hundred years.

CONCLUSION

Ancient musical instruments are rare and it is unlikely that it will ever be possible to have more than tantalising and partial knowledge of the history of side drums in the centuries before 1700.

The date of the Drake drum is enigmatic. Its size, elaborate nail patterns and the mark cut into the shell which may be the number thirteen and so link it with the thirteen drums bought for Drake and Hawkins' expedition in 1595 all suggest that the drum belongs to the time of the first Sir Francis Drake. Yet the seventeenth century style of the coat of arms on the drum contradicts this unless it was indeed added later. Neither family records nor scientific dating techniques can resolve the question.

Although much less famous than the drum the eight Drake flags are unique. The two splendid Royal Standards certainly belong to Queen Elizabeth I's reign and to Sir Francis Drake. The six military Colours are the same size as the square Royal flag and were assumed by Drake's eighteenth century descendants to belong to him.

Perhaps the drum, the standards and colours really do all belong to the sixteenth century and were preserved by Sir Francis Drake's brother Thomas on his return from their very last sea voyage together. Although the mystery remains these splendid treasures link us across four centuries to the lives of craftsmen, soldiers and to a heroic English sailor, Sir Francis Drake.

NOTES

1. Christie, Manson and Woods, 1966. Plymouth Museum archive. National Trust archive.
2. Montagu, 1976, p.23.
3. Plymouth Museum archive.
4. Letters in Plymouth Museum archive.
5. Courtesy of Mr M Grayson, Derriford Hospital, Plymouth.
6. Blades and Montagu, 1976, p.6; Farmer nd; Finlay 1953; Gutmann 1983.
7. Quoted in Blades, 1970.
8. Purchas' Pilgrims, Hakluyt Society, 1905, vol 19.
9. Sir Francis Drake Revived, 1626. Hakluyt Society, 1932, p.263.
10. Papers relating to the Spanish War, 1585–1587. J Corbett, ed. Naval Records Society. 1898.
11. Andrews, 1972, p.55.
12. Andrews, 1972, p.55.
13. Andrews, 1972, p.60.
14. Andrews, 1972, pp 35–48.
15. Guttman, 1983.
16. National Army Museum Catalogue, 1988. Personal communications, Maurice Byrne.
17. Drake Papers. Devon Record Office, 346M/F571–587, c.1682.
18. Drake Papers. Devon Record Office, 346M/E616.
19. Borg, 1975; Royal Armouries archive.
20. Fletcher, 1976; Klein, et al., 1986.
21. Plymouth Museum archive.
22. Worth, 1884.
23. National Trust and Plymouth Museum archive.
24. Drake Papers. Devon Record Office. 346M/E616.
25. Perrin, 1922.
26. Andrews, 1972, p.56
27. Peachey and Prince, 1991; Elton, 1659. A fifth English Civil War flag was identified in 1994 at Antony House, Cornwall, belonging to the Carew-Pole family.
28. Boynton, 1971.
29. Andrews, 1972, p.233, 234; Wilson 1986, p.15.
30. **1569**–Devon Muster Roll. PRO/SP12/52 and Typescript in DRO.D:3205. **1625**–Devon Session Order. DRO.1148 M.Add 18/1. **1629**–Officers at Muster, Foot. PRO.SP16 /150/76; Stannaries, PRO.SP16/153/113,114. **1631**–Officers at Muster, Foot. PRO.SP16/202/55; Horse, PRO.SP16/199/ 29,32,22. **1633**–Muster list. PRO.SP. Dom.C.I.vol 241, no.55. **1638**–Officers at Muster, Stannaries. DRO. 219/47/2. **1645**–Drake regiment of Horse. PRO. SP.28.139. part 16. **1662**–Stannaries order. DRO.48/14/152/1. **1697**–Militia list. Brit.Mus.Egerton, 1626.
31. Ede–Borrett, 1984, 1987, 1989. Ede-Borrett mistakenly assumed in 1987 that Colonel Sir John Drake was a member of the Buckland Abbey Drake family and dated the flags to 1633. Burke, 1884; Vivian, 1896; Worth 1884.
32. Walrond, 1897, prints the 1633 and 1697 Militia lists.
33. Milne, 1893.
34. Glen Foard, personal communications.
35. British Library catalogue, 1977.
36. Andrews, 1972, p.86.
37. Bray, 1838; press cuttings and letters, Plymouth Museum archive.
38. Ditmas, 1973; Hunt, 1871.

BIBLIOGRAPHY

AITKEN, M.J., 1990 *Science Based Dating in Archaeology*, Longman, London.

ANDREWS, K.R., 1972 *The Last Voyage of Drake and Hawkins*, Cambridge, published for the Haklyut Society.

ANON, c.1590 *The True Portraiture of the Valiant English Soldiers in their Proceedings to the Wars,* Pepys Library, Magdalene College, Cambridge. Revised STC 20/26.7.

ARBEAU, Thoinot, 1588 *Orchesography – A Treatise in the form of a dialogue whereby all manner of persons may easily acquire and practise the honourable exercise of dancing,* Various English editions: including Beaumont, C.W., 1925, London; Dover Press, New York, 1967.

AYLOFFE, Sir Joseph, 1776 'Some Ancient English Paintings at Cowdry', *Archaeologia, III,* .London 1776.

BAILLIE, M.G., 1982 *Tree Ring Dating*, Croom Helm, London.

BAINES, A., 1966 *European and American Musical Instruments,* Batsford, London.

BLADES, J., 1970 *Percussion Instruments and their History,* Faber & Faber, London.

BLADES, J. & MONTAGU, J., 1976 *Early Percussion Instruments,* Oxford University Press.

BORG, A., 1975 'Dating a Dutch Drum' in *Country Life,* February 27, 1975. 490.

BOYNTON, L., 1971 *The Elizabethan Militia 1558–1638,* David & Charles, Newton Abbot.

BRAY, A.E., 1838 *Traditions, legends, superstitions and sketches of Devonshire on the borders of the Tamar and Tavy ...* in a series of letters to Robert Southey, Vol. 2. 172–3.

BRITISH LIBRARY, 1977 *Sir Francis Drake. An Exhibition to Commemorate Francis Drake's Voyage around the World 1577–1580.* British Museum Publications, London.

BURKE, 1884 *General Armoury.*

CHRISTIE, MANSON & WOODS, 1966 *Appraisal of Drake's Drum,* Plymouth City Museum Archive.

CORBETT, J.S., 1899 *Drake and the Tudor Navy.* Vol. 1 & 2. Longmans Green & Co., London.

DITMAS, E.M.R., 1973 'The Legend of Drake's Drum' *West Country Folklore No.6.* The Toucan Press, Guernsey.

EDE–BORRETT, S., 1980 Letter in Plymouth City Museum, *Buckland file 6/7/02D*, About the Drake colours.

EDE–BORRETT, S., 1984 'The Drake Colours' in *Military Modelling,* April 1984, 288.

EDE–BORRETT, S., 1987 *Flags of the English Civil Wars,* part 1, 12. Raider Games, Leeds.

EDE–BORRETT, S., 1989 'The Drake Colours' in *Journal of the Society for Army Historical Research,* Vol.LXVII, No 270, 121.

ELIOTT–DRAKE, Lady, 1911 *The Family and Heirs of Sir Francis Drake*, London, 1911.

ELTON, R, 1659 *Compleat Body of the Art Military.*

FARMER, H.G., n.d. *Military Music* p.23 (illustration of Drummer)

FINLAY, I.F., 1953 'Musical Instruments in 17th Century Dutch Paintings' in *Galpin Society Journal* VI, 52–69.

FLETCHER, J., 1976 'Oak Antiques Tree Ring Analysis' in *Antique Collecting and Antique Finder,* October 1976, 9–11.

FOARD, G., in preparation. *Ensigns and their Flags during the English Civil Wars.*

GUTMANN, V., 1983 *Trommeln und Tambourmajorstöcke in der sammlung alter Musikinstrumente des Historischen Museums,* Basel.

HOPE, W.H. St John, 1919 *Cowdray and Easebourne Priory in the County of Sussex,* 59–65, London.

HUNT, R., 1871 *Popular Romances of the West of England,* London.

KING, C., 1952 'The Kings Flags and some others' in *Mariner's Mirror,* Vol. 38, 84–105.

KLEIN, P., MEHRINGER, H. & BAUCH, J., 1986 'Dendrochronological and Wood Biological Investigations on String Instruments' in *Holzforshung,* Vol. 40, No. 4, 197–203.

LLOYD, C. AND THURLEY, S., 1990 Henry VIII: *Images of a Tudor King,* Phaidon Press & Historic Royal Palaces Agency, London.

LUMPKIN, H., 1960 'The Pictures of Henry VIII's Army in Cotton Manuscript Augustus III' in *Journal of the Arms and Armour Society,* Vol. III, 145–170.

MARKHAM, G, 1625 *The Soldiers Accidence.*

MERSENNE, Marin, 1636 *Harmonie Universelle,* The Books on Instruments,. Translation by R. Chapman, Martinus Nijhoff, The Hague, 1957, 550.

MILNE, S.M, 1893 *Standards and Colours of the Army ...1661–1881.*

MONTAGU, J., 1976 *Making Early Percussion Instruments.* Music Department, Oxford University Press.

NATIONAL ARMY MUSEUM 1988 *Follow the Drum*: Exhibition Catalogue, London.

NATIONAL TRUST, 1991, *Buckland Abbey, Devon.*

NEWBOLT, H., 1932 *My World as in My Time.* Faber & Faber, London

NOYES, A., *Collected Poems.*

OMAN, C., 1937 *A History of the Art of War in the Sixteenth Century.* Methuen, London.

PEACHEY, S. & PRINCE, L., 1991 *English Civil War Flags and Colours: 1. English Foot.* Partizan Press, Leigh–on–Sea, Essex.

PERRIN, W G, 1922 *British Flags.* London.

PRAETORIUS, Michael, 1619 *Syntagma Musicum* Wolfenbattel, reprinted Kassel, 1931.

REMNANT, M., 1989 *Musical Instruments: An Illustrated History from Antiquity to the Present.* Batsford, London.

RIJKSMUSEUM AMSTERDAM, 1976 *All the Paintings of the Rijksmuseum Amsterdam.*

SADIE, S. (ed), 1980 *The New Grove Dictionary of Music and Musicians: Side Drum* Vol. 5, Macmillan, London, 644–648.

SOUTHEY, R., 1895 *English Seamen: Howard, Clifford, Hawkins, Drake, Cavendish, 1895.* (Essays written before 1843)

TINCEY, J, 1988 *The Armada Campaign, 1588 with illustrations by R.Hook.* Osprey Elite Series, London.

VIVIAN, J.L., 1896 *The Visitations of Devon.* Comprising the Herald's Visitations of 1531, 1564 and 1620 with additions by Lt Col. J.L. Vivian. Exeter. Privately printed in parts 1894–96.

WALROND, H., 1897 *Historical Records of the Ist Devon Militia (4th Battalion, The Devonshire Regiment)*, London.

WILSON, T, 1986 *Flags at Sea.* National Maritime Museum, London.

WORTH, R.N., 1884 'Sir Francis Drake; His Origin, Arms and Dealings with the Plymouth Corporation' in *Transactions of the Devonshire Association,* Vol.XVI, 505–552.

ACKNOWLEDGEMENTS

Of the many people who have enthusiastically responded to my questions I would especially like to thank Mr Jeremy Montagu, Faculty of Music, University of Oxford, and Mr Maurice Byrne, Galpin Society, for help and advice on side drums; and Mr Glen Foard, Northampton, for much enlightenment about seventeenth century flags and military practice.

I am most grateful to Dr Mary Wolffe, University of Exeter, and Dr Mark Stoyle, University of Southampton for information on seventeenth century militia and the Civil War; and to Professor Mike Baillie, University of Belfast for dendrochronology references.

Professor Joyce Youings, Glen Foard and Jeremy Montagu have kindly commented on the text which was typed by Janie Percival and Wendy Penwill. The scale drawing of the Drake Drum was specially drawn by Richard Fisher from measurements by Cynthia Gaskell Brown.

Staff from museums in Basel, Dublin, Edinburgh and London; libraries in Bristol, London and Plymouth and the Devon Record Offices have all assisted with great goodwill. The help of colleagues from the National Trust, Plymouth Museum and Art Gallery and Mount Edgcumbe House has been much appreciated.

This book is dedicated to the late James Barber whose quiet scholarship and steady friendship is greatly missed.

THE DRAKE FAMILY INHERITANCE

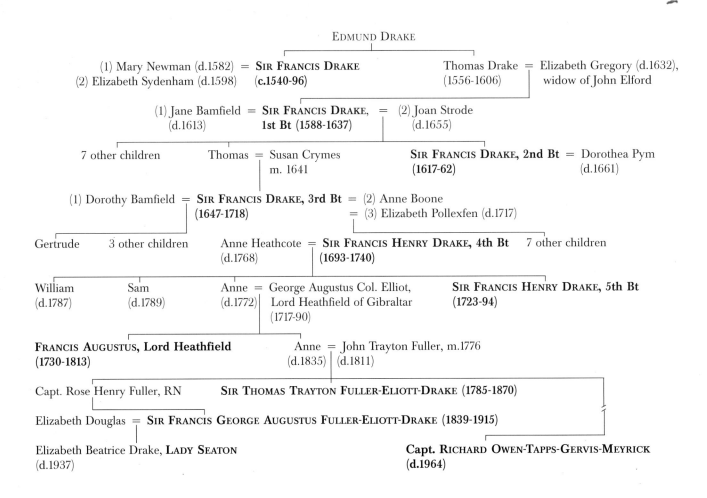

EDMUND DRAKE

(1) Mary Newman (d.1582) = **SIR FRANCIS DRAKE**   Thomas Drake = Elizabeth Gregory (d.1632),
(2) Elizabeth Sydenham (d.1598)   **(c.1540-96)**   (1556-1606)   widow of John Elford

(1) Jane Bamfield = **SIR FRANCIS DRAKE,** = (2) Joan Strode
(d.1613)   **1st Bt (1588-1637)**   (d.1655)

7 other children   Thomas = Susan Crymes   **SIR FRANCIS DRAKE, 2nd Bt** = Dorothea Pym
   m. 1641   **(1617-62)**   (d.1661)

(1) Dorothy Bamfield = **SIR FRANCIS DRAKE, 3rd Bt** = (2) Anne Boone
   (1647-1718)   = (3) Elizabeth Pollexfen (d.1717)

Gertrude   3 other children   Anne Heathcote = **SIR FRANCIS HENRY DRAKE, 4th Bt**   7 other children
   (d.1768)   **(1693-1740)**

William   Sam   Anne = George Augustus Col. Elliot,   **SIR FRANCIS HENRY DRAKE, 5th Bt**
(d.1787)   (d.1789)   (d.1772) Lord Heathfield of Gibraltar   **(1723-94)**
      (1717-90)

FRANCIS AUGUSTUS, Lord Heathfield   Anne = John Trayton Fuller, m.1776
(1730-1813)   (d.1835) (d.1811)

Capt. Rose Henry Fuller, RN   **SIR THOMAS TRAYTON FULLER-ELIOTT-DRAKE (1785-1870)**

Elizabeth Douglas = **SIR FRANCIS GEORGE AUGUSTUS FULLER-ELIOTT-DRAKE (1839-1915)**

Elizabeth Beatrice Drake, **LADY SEATON**   **Capt. RICHARD OWEN-TAPPS-GERVIS-MEYRICK**
(d.1937)   **(d.1964)**

42